WEL/LO

A Dream of the Land

A Dream of the Land

PHOTOGRAPHS AND INTRODUCTION BY JOHN T HANSELL M.A.

"I can't imagine that many books have been written that contain so few words as this one, but does it? Look again. My language is a visual one, my voice is a camera, and the images I make and print speak a language more eloquent than I could speak in words. I am a self confessed dreamer who loves the landscape and I make images about special moments in time that I have experienced within it.

This is a book in which the words will be different for each person that reads it, and they will change again and again each time it is read."

John T Hansell M.A,1998

Published in Great Britain by Hansart, 2006.
©2006 Hansart
Introduction Text and Photographs: ©2005 John T Hansell M.A.

www.johnhansell.com

Cover Photograph: Holkham Bay, Norfolk

ISBN   0-9552711-0-X

A tribute to John T Hansell M.A.

"Never to be forgotten"

This book has been published by John's immediate family (Jane, Tim, Jo, Na and Angus) as a tribute to an exceptionally talented and inspirational husband, father, father-in-law, friend and photographer, who was loved and highly regarded by all who had the good fortune to share in his life.

Introduction

John's interest in photography began at the age of just eleven and later became his profession, with him spending thirty years as a forensic photographer with the Norfolk police force. Photographing the landscape provided a peaceful escape from the crime and horror of his demanding career. Upon retirement from the police force, aged forty-nine, John turned to lecturing photography at the Norfolk college where, over the course of the next nine years, he inspired a future generation of photographers.

During the course of John's life his work received much acclaim across a number of different media and artistic channels:

- a number of his photographs have been used as covers for novels and published by the likes of Penguin and Random House;

- his work has been featured in publications such as SLR Photography, Art East and the Eastern Daily Press weekend magazine;

- he won the Kentmere prize for Photography in 1995 and 1997;

- he was featured in an Award-winning Documentary in 1993 on Anglia TV, filmed by Alan Neale;

- his work has been displayed at a number of both dedicated, and also as part of mixed, exhibitions, as a result of which his work has been bought for private collections all over the world;

- in addition to his reputation as a leading landscape photographer, he has also had other works published by the Architectural Association and has photographed a number of prestigious properties on behalf of leading estate agents in East Anglia.

The introduction below is an excerpt taken from work submitted by John for his M.A. in Photography at De Montfort University, Leicester and aptly tells the story, in John's own words, of his introduction to photography:

"Looking back on one's life you realise that it has been shaped by fate; that curious chance happening that on reflection altered the route you took. What would have happened if you made a different decision on 'that day'? Been late? Took a different approach? And so on. Of course, nobody can answer that question and you can only wonder. I have spent my professional life photographing my fellow man's wrong doings and yet if I am truthful it was a personal wrong doing that led me down that path.

When I was ten years old I lied about my age to get a job as a 'paperboy', [the legal age was eleven at that time] for which I was paid ten shillings a week to deliver newspapers around a local housing estate and collect the money on Saturdays. On the Saturday before Christmas that first year when I collected the money, people gave me a 'Christmas tip' a shilling here, a half-a-crown there and so on and at the end of my round I had over three pounds to buy something with. That day was over forty years ago and yet I remember it as clearly as yesterday, that day shaped the rest of my life!

I caught a bus to town that afternoon, my pockets bulging with coins; three pounds would buy many things a small boy yearned for. I could buy the chemistry set or microscope I so wanted but I was hoping to get them for Christmas, well more than hope, as I had been peeking in the parcels hidden behind my Mum's wardrobe. I had such a choice that I wandered round and round the many toy shops. One of them was WHSmith's, which in those days had a large toy department as well as the largest book shop in town. I wasn't that keen on reading at ten, but as I wandered through the display of books I spotted one that drew me to it, "The Boy's Book of Hobbies". I lifted the book from the shelf and flicked through the pages. I had found, what was for me, the Holy Grail.

I was a kid who loved to do things, to experiment, to explore – I was interested in everything. I was different to the rest of the family. Don't get me wrong, I came from a working class family whose needs were few. My mother worked particularly hard to ensure we were always well turned out and wanted for very little; she really cared for us. Mother had, in her words, been regarded as a cripple in her childhood and had received no education. She could not read or write and so I acquired the skill of teaching myself all those interesting things I wanted to know about and which she couldn't help me with.

I purchased the book and couldn't wait to get home to delve into this veritable treasure chest of things to make and do; it contained the answers to where I went wrong with all those exciting projects I had attempted so far in my life, like - Why did the homing pigeons I bought from the boy down the road for a shilling, go home to him when I let them out? Why when I stepped into the canoe I so lovingly built and covered with roofing felt did I go straight through it and end up standing on the river bed? The answers were all there together with exciting chapters on camping, cycling, chemistry, microscopy, astronomy, woodwork and the one chapter that transfixed me totally, photography. We didn't own a camera so I had never really thought about it; this was magic, it had to be. I still think it's magic after all these years. I read that chapter over and over until I knew all about cameras, shutters and apertures, films, developing and printing and much more and yet I had never even handled a camera. I made countless journeys down to Mr. Goodchild's, the local photographic studio and shop, to peer through the window at all those magical things I had read about.

My eleventh birthday was at the end of January and my parents and relatives all gave me money which, together with what I earned delivering papers, meant I had enough to buy a "Coronet Flash Camera" and small packets of developer, fixer and contact printing paper to process the first photographs I would have ever taken. I had nobody to help me. I remember it cost nine shillings then for a film and two packets of five flashbulbs; nearly a weeks wages for a paperboy. I soon shot off the ten flash pictures and used the remaining two to photograph "Prince", my dog, outside.

We didn't have anywhere that would provide the complete darkness I would need to see-saw the film through the dishes of chemicals and I was too impatient to wait for darkness to fall. I found that if I took a few items out, I could just about cram myself into the food cupboard; it seemed to be quite dark in there when the door was shut. My birthday money had not stretched to proper developing dishes or a thermometer, so I guessed the temperature and used mother's enamelled rice pudding dishes to do the processing in. After a minute or two of see-sawing the long length of film through the developer my arms were aching and I realised to my horror that I could actually see what I was doing; the cupboard was not light tight.

The film was "fogged" but I was still excited, I could see negative images on the film through the fogging. It had actually worked, the book was right. I had performed my first piece of magic! That I had fogged the film was nobody's fault but mine, the important thing for me was that it worked and I would get it right next time. I had no money left and father thought it was a complete waste of money anyway and that when I could afford another film I should take it to the chemist like everybody else – photography was not for the likes of us!

I was upset about it and my mother produced nine shillings which she could ill afford, and came up with a proposal: a lady living down the road had just had a baby and she would like some "flash" pictures taken of it; she would pay the nine shillings for the film and flashbulbs and a little extra for some prints if they came out. This was to be my second and last chance. I agreed with mother that if I didn't get it right this time I would give up the processing side of photography; we simply couldn't afford it.

I got it right.

I went to a secondary school and they had a photography club which I joined. I am still in contact with two of the other lads who were members - one is a photojournalist and the other a television news cameraman – they were each a year older than me and scooped up the only two photography jobs likely to come up in the area for years.

What was I to do? I wanted to be a photographer; there were no college courses in photography then but even if there had been we could not have afforded it. For a while it looked as if I would have to find the sort of job which a secondary education had equipped me for i.e. a labourer, an apprenticeship, shop worker or a clerk if I was lucky. Then fate played its second card; the brother of a friend of mine had joined the police force at the age of 16 as a "Cadet". I spoke to him; it looked exciting and he told me they had a photographic department.

I wrote off and was called to the large new local police headquarters for an interview. I was told that you could not join as a photographer; in fact they only had one and he was based at their Force Headquarters in Norwich, he came out to take photographs when required, anyway you would have to train as a police officer first. I took the decision to join and was taken to an empty room with a measuring scale on the wall to ascertain my height. On the door it said "Photographic Department". When I asked about it I was told it was something designed for the future. As it turned out I was the future; I was to set up that department and run it for thirty years of my life."

John T Hansell, 1998

Holkham Bay - Norfolk

A Beach on Lewis - Outer Hebrides

The Standing Stones at Callanish - Lewis

Mull - The Western Isles

Leaving Mull

Eilean Donan Castle - Scotland

The Angel of the North

New Scottish Parliament Building - Edinburgh

Ocean Point - Leith, Edinburgh

Lindisfarne

Lindisfarne Castle (The Holy Island)

Walkers and Dramatic Sky - Cumbria

Castlerigg - Cumbria

Helvellyn from Hartsop

Catstye Cam from above Hartsop - The Lake District

Brotherswater from above Hartsop - Lake District

Blencathra and Grazing Sheep - Cumbria

Tree and Sheep - Cumbria

Connemara

On the Beara Pass - Southern Ireland

Fenced Mountains - Connemara

The Dolmen - Southern Ireland

A Road Through Connemara

White Rock Strand - Northern Ireland

The Giant's Causeway - Northern Ireland

Castle of the Winds - Snowdonia

The Cantilever Stone - Snowdonia

Rylstone Fell - Christmas Day 2000

A Green Lane near Horton in Ribblesdale

Fountains Fell

Pendle Hill from Fleets Moor

Rylstone Cross

From Rylstone Fell

Road Across Fleets Moor - Yorkshire Dales

Wind Turbines at Chelker Reservoir - Yorkshire Dales

Staithes

Pen-y-ghent - Yorkshire Dales

Gordale Scar - Malham

Robin Hood's Bay

Lone Tree near Kinder Scout - Derbyshire

Edale, Derbyshire from the Pennine Way

Stones on Kinder Scout - Derbyshire

Kinder Low from Kinder Scout - Derbyshire

Standing Stone - Avebury

Stonehenge

Six Minutes past Twelve - Canary Wharf

Canary Wharf Tube Station

Who needs a car? - Dungeness

St. Mary-in-the-Marsh - Romney Marsh

Heading for Westminster

Paris - October 2004

Venice

The Grand Canal - Venice

The Wash

The Great Ouse and Sugar Beet Factory - King's Lynn - Circa 1985

Spring in a Beech Wood at Houghton - Norfolk

Fenland Allotment in the Mist

Field near Downham Market

People Watching

The Silver Tree

Edge of a Wood in the Mist

Keeper's Lane - Castle Rising

Wootton Woods

The First Morning of the New Millennium 01.01.2000

Tree and Sheep in the Mist near Sedgeford - Norfolk

Tree on Peddars Way near Bircham

Peddars Way near Fring - Norfolk

Bircham Mill and Small White Clouds

Farm Track and Mushroom Cloud - Norfolk

Bird Scarer in a Field near Fring - Norfolk

Setting Sun and Rising Mist near Fring - Norfolk

The Old Jetty - Snettisham, Norfolk

The Old Jetty - Snettisham, Norfolk (2)

The Bait Digger

The Bait Diggers (Snettisham, Norfolk)

A Stroll - Heacham, Norfolk

Boat on Snettisham Beach

Three Winter Trees - Sandringham

Tree Shadow near Shernborne

Old Hunstanton Beach - Winter

Beach Textures - Old Hunstanton

Hunstanton Cliffs and Large White Clouds

Rock and Pool - Old Hunstanton

Beach Huts at Old Hunstanton

Bird Watcher (Jane) - Old Hunstanton

The Mussel Beds - Old Hunstanton

Fence Post and Marram Grass - Old Hunstanton

The End of the Holiday

Hunstanton Pier (destroyed by gales)

Two Terns and a Cormorant - Old Hunstanton

Drifting Sand - Old Hunstanton

Holme Beach - Receding Tide

Fenced Dunes - Holme

Oyster Catchers - Holme, Norfolk

Path to Holme Beach

Holme Groynes (Cross Processed Film)

Posts and Shadows - Holme Beach

Sandstorm - Holme Beach

Four Swans on Holme Beach

Holme, Norfolk

Holme, Norfolk (2)

Board Walk between Holme and Thornham

Beach Fence at Holme

Lone Tree near Thornham

Thornham Marsh

Boat and Tree Trunks - Thornham Marsh

Spring Tide - Thornham Marsh

Tree Trunks and Sluice Gate - Thornham

Thornham - Changing Weather

White Boat - Thornham

Reed Bed - Titchwell Nature Reserve

RSPB Reserve at Titchwell

Burnham Thorpe - Nelson's Birthplace

Brancaster Beach - Late on a Summer's Evening

Kite Flying - Brancaster Beach

A Stroll on Brancaster Beach

Post, Gull and Lone Walker - Brancaster Beach (October)

Rocks on Brancaster Beach

Walkers on Brancaster Beach

Dropping in on Brancaster

Brancaster - A Sunday Afternoon - Late Winter

Beach and Groynes - Brancaster

Groynes (2) Brancaster Beach

Post on Brancaster Beach

Groynes on Brancaster Beach

Cottage on the Norfolk Coastal Path near Brancaster

Dog Walkers - Brancaster Beach

Still Water - Brancaster Staithe

Boats and Gull - Brancaster Staithe

Two Boats - Brancaster Staithe

Lone Boat - Brancaster Staithe

Two Boats - Brancaster Staithe (2)

Gull and Dinghy - Brancaster Staithe

Twilight - Brancaster Staithe

Yacht Tenders - Flood Tide, Brancaster Staithe

Boats and Gull - Brancaster Staithe (2)

Dinghy Masts - Brancaster Staithe

Burnham Overy Mill

Burnham Overy Staithe

Fishing - Overy Staithe

Burnham Overy Staithe (2)

Alone - Gun Hill Beach, Norfolk

Anchor on Holkham Beach

Clouds over Holkham Bay

Anchor on Holkham Beach

Clouds over Holkham Bay

Holkham Beach - Winter

Follow the Dog - Holkham Beach (Christmas)

Tree Branch on Holkham Beach

Goose and Deer - Holkham Park, Norfolk

Post on Holkham Beach

Last Four Beach Huts and Walker - Wells

Beach Huts at Wells

Wells - Groynes and Markers

The Lifeboat Station - Wells

Walkers on Wells Beach - Late Winter

Beach Huts and High Tide - Wells

Cley - The Mill in the Middle

Cley Mill - Norfolk

Cley Mill and Large White Clouds

Cley - Creek and Boat

Cley Mill through the Reed Bed

Cley Mill and Norfolk Reeds

Low Tide - Blakeney Point

Seals at Blakeney Point - Norfolk

Geese over Cley Marsh

Two Boats and a Path - Salthouse

Landing - Salthouse Beach, Norfolk

A Stroll - Salthouse, Norfolk

Weybourne Beach and Cliffs - Norfolk

Covehithe

Sunset and Pink Footed Geese - Hunstanton